How Can I Talk to God?

Children's Christian Prayer Books

BABY PROFESSOR

EDUCATION KIDS

Speedy Publishing LLC
40 E. Main St. #1156
Newark, DE 19711
www.speedypublishing.com

How to talk to God? Is it possible to talk to God today?

Let's take a look at meaningful ways of talking to God. Read on and strengthen your connection with the Lord.

Learning how to communicate with God strengthens our spiritual and personal relationship with Him. Talking to God is possible for all people, of all spiritual preferences and religions.

Talking to God requires sincerity and honesty. We should be ready to admit and confess our wrongdoings, our hopes, and where we are confused. God knows we are not perfect, so we don't have to pretend we are. Be truthful at all times.

God offers us a personal relationship as he invites us to draw closer to God. This relationship can be strengthened by our actions and prayers. Our prayers are our words to God. When we pray, we speak intentionally with Him.

When we talk with God in prayer, we make ourselves open to God's response. Prayers move mountains—not because we are strong, but because God is. Here are the tips to make our prayers worthwhile.

Set a time to
pray every day.

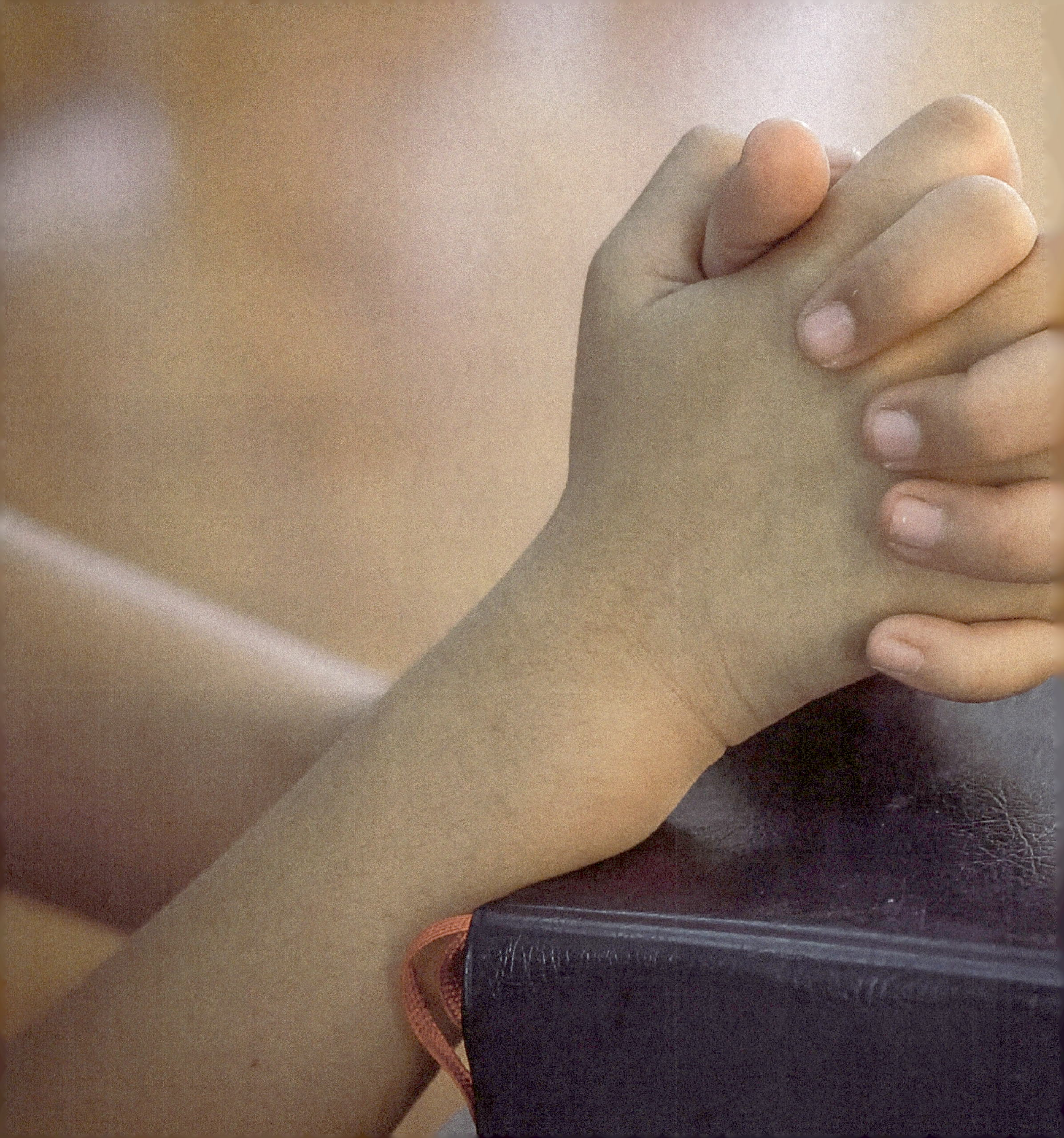

Make an appointment with God every day. Be a consistent person of prayer. Plan a schedule of prayer each day, although we can actually pray at any time.

The Bible tells us to pray always. Our prayers are formal ways of communicating to God. Prayer can be said any time and in any place. This is so because God is omnipresent. He is always with us and listening to us.

Specify a Place
of Prayer. Find
a place in your
home where you
can stay focused
while praying.

Although we can pray and talk to God anywhere, it's still important to develop an attitude of prayer. Turn off the radio and go where people will not try to talk with you. You may choose to pray in a quiet room or in the park—wherever you want to as long as your focus is on your prayer.

We can talk to
God as we talk to
a friend—a wise,
patient friend
who wants the
good for us.

Speak to God with a trusting attitude. Kneel, sit, or stand with your hands held up as you pray—not to show off to others, but to show your attention to God. Don't make your prayers complicated. Talk to God with all due respect and adoration. He understands what you have been through. Talk with God, now.

Prayer can deepen our relationship with God. When we talk with him regularly, we can see more easily what he is doing and what he wants us to do in the world.

Knowing God should be our first action as faithful people. We can know Him well through His word. Reading God's words is a means of knowing the truth.

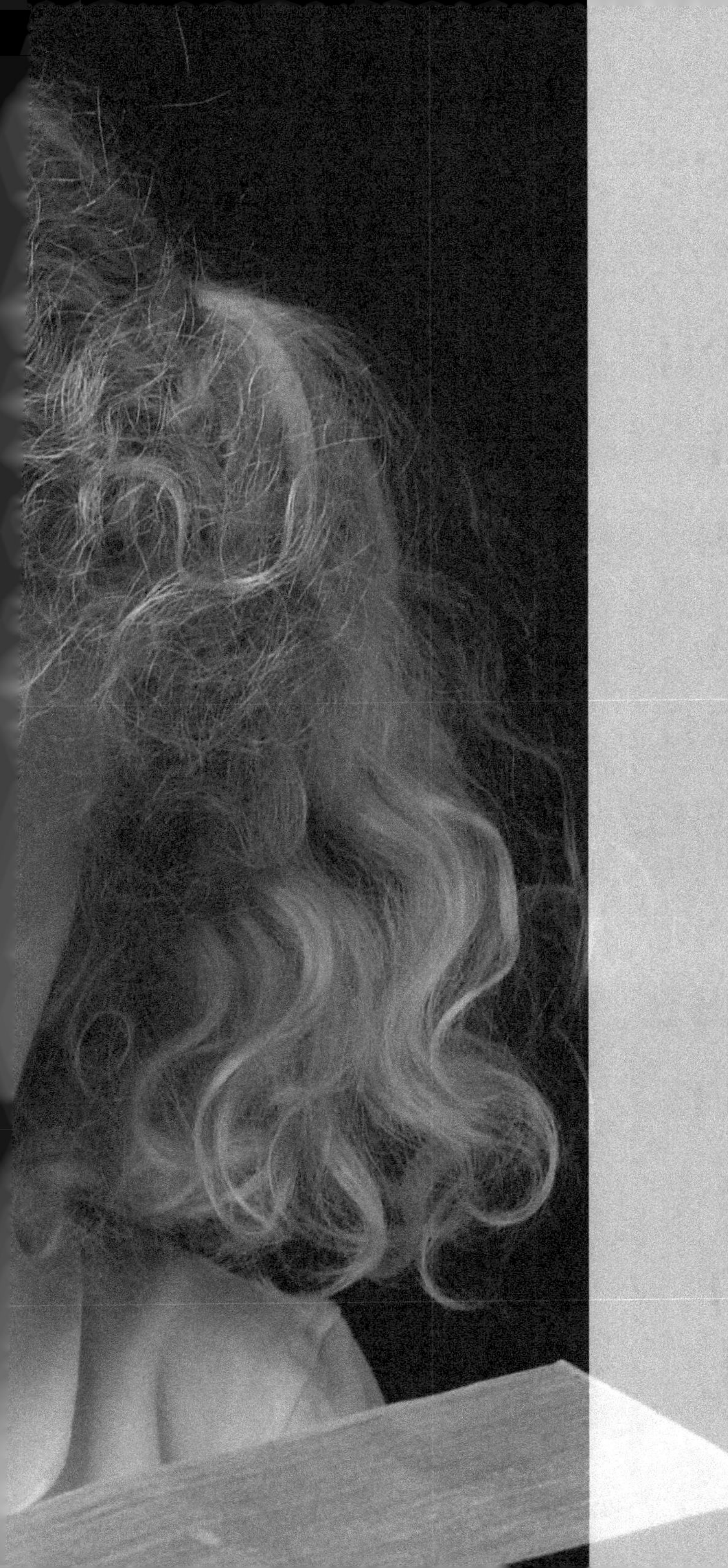

Create a
Prayer List.

A prayer list helps you remember who and what you want to talk with God about. This helps keep you focused and open for God's response. Keep a prayer journal. Don't just pray for your own needs: include other people in your prayer list.

If you are by
yourself, say
your prayers
aloud. This helps
you focus.

Stay focused when you pray. God can hear us in our silent prayers, but speaking aloud to Him can help keep our mind from wandering while we pray.

Visit

BABY PROFESSOR
EDUCATION KIDS

www.BabyProfessorBooks.com

to download Free Baby Professor eBooks
and view our catalog of new and exciting
Children's Books